Getting to Know You
Experiencing Boundary County Through Its People

BOULDER CREEK ACADEMY SERVICE LEARNING STUDENTS

Green Withy Press

Copyright © 2015

Boulder Creek Academy Service Learning Students

All rights reserved.

ISBN: 1514336901
ISBN-13: 978-1514336908

Green Withy Press
278 Cardinal Lane
Bonners Ferry, ID 83805

Editors-in-Chief: Billy Bowers, Alan Viola

Writing/Editing: Jackson Smaldone, Maggie Walker-Petrozzini, Charles Hunter

Photography: Andrew Yanishevski, Meredith Winters, Connor Brockmeyer

Interviews: Dylan Thompson, Christopher Comstock, Michael Herkelrath

Marketing: Sam Goodman, Michael G., Logan Merlina, Davis Young, Andre Vu

Special Contributors: Mitchell Goss, Krystal F., Morgan Rothschild

Advisors: Valerie Thompson, Willow Feller

CONTENTS

HOWARD KENT……………………………………………………	1
GARY AITKEN…………………………………………………...	3
PHYLLIS COLLYER……………………………………………...	5
RICHARD HOLLENBECK…………………………………………	7
ELSIE HOLLENBECK……………………………………………..	9
DARRELL KERBY………………………………………………...	11
SANDY ASHWORTH…………………………………………….	13
RON SMITH………………………………………………………	15
CAROLYN TESTA………………………………………………..	17
TIM WILSON……………………………………………………..	19
BARB RAWLINGS………………………………………………..	21
TIM DILLIN………………………………………………………	23
ALVA BAKER…………………………………………………….	25
SUE WILSON…………………………………………………….	27
DAVID MCINTOSH……………………………………………...	29
JUDY DIRKS……………………………………………………..	31
DAN DINNING…………………………………………………..	33

You are holding a book of modern history, designed and created by students of Boulder Creek Academy in conjunction with influential members of the Bonners Ferry community. At Boulder Creek, students are part of a volunteer-based community initiative called Service Learning. After exploring several options, as well as the history of Boundary County, they decided that they would like to know more about current members of the community.

In this book, you'll find articles covering a group of key Boundary County citizens. Each person was identified by others in the area as important or influential to the life of the community as a whole. You will also discover a diverse group, representing a variety of people who together impact North Idaho for the better. While they do not make up all of the people who enrich Boundary County, they represent a cross section of good people who have helped us learn more about the little town that is our temporary home.

We hope you enjoy this unique glimpse into the Bonners Ferry community and the amazing people who make it what it is today.

-Boulder Creek Academy Service Learning Community Initiative

Howard Kent, a retired history teacher from Bonners Ferry, takes pride in his work and in the heritage his family established in this community. As our local historian, he researches for the Boundary County Museum, provides tours, and writes documents about the county's history. While at the museum, he has written the *History of Boundary County* (1808-2013).

Howard's grandfather came to Bonners Ferry in 1893, and his family remained in the same house until 1953. When the family later moved across the highway on the South Hill to a new house, Howard often felt "homesick" and returned to his old home for visits. He lived less than a quarter mile away from the old place so Howard says, "I did not have to go far to deal with my homesickness." He also vividly recalls his father rowing a boat through the window of his grandmother's house during the terrible flood of '48.

Howard's mother enlisted him in the Navy before he turned eighteen, and he was later stationed in Washington. He went on to attend the University of Idaho on the G.I. bill, deciding against re-enlistment in the Navy. By the time the Vietnam war heated up, Howard had a family; he was not called back to serve.

He returned to Bonners Ferry and worked at Safeway until a science teaching job opened up at Valley View Elementary, then later instructed high school social studies. In all, Howard taught for thirty-two years and gives compliments to his wife, Donna, who was a teacher for forty years. As a BFHS graduate of 1960, one of Howard's many committees provides scholarships for local college-bound students.

Howard loves the landscapes, environment, and small town comfort of Bonners Ferry. The hustle and bustle of city life holds no appeal for him. He recognizes many recent changes, particularly changes in the downtown area, as he watches local variety and hardware stores going out of business. Aside from that, he believes Bonners Ferry has changed for the better. He sees it becoming more of a retirement community and hopes that it will forever retain the small-town atmosphere he loves.

Working hard to preserve Bonners Ferry history, Howard's ultimate goal is for locals and newcomers alike to always recognize and celebrate the unique spirit of his beloved community.

Gary Aitken was born in Spokane, Washington and moved to Bonners Ferry at age three. He went to North Side and Valley View Elementary schools, Boundary County Junior High, and then graduated from Riverside High School. Much remains the same in Bonners Ferry since he was a child; the town is still free and friendly, and a great place to raise kids. It's a place, he says, where he and others can make a difference in the lives of their children through coaching and volunteering in the community.

One aspect of Boundary County that Gary believes has changed for the better is interracial relations. In grade school, Gary said that he was involved in many fights that sprang from racial tension. He was proud to stick up for his heritage. But today, with improved relations, the Kootenai Tribe works with the rest of the community because, as Gary says, "Of course we don't always agree, but we can always agree to move forward. Eventually, it's time to stop fighting and go around a brick wall."

Currently, Gary serves as Chairperson for the Kootenai Tribe, as well as a member of the Kootenai Valley Resource Initiative, a community-based collaborative between stakeholders representing the county, the city, and the Kootenai Tribe. The KVRI's mission is "to improve coordination of local, state, federal and tribal programs to restore and maintain social, cultural, economic and natural resources." Gary takes pride in the collaborative effort. "After all," he says, "there's something about this area that people cherish. It's our community. We want to raise our kids here. How can we make it better?"

Gary believes that we should study our ecosystem, considering what he calls a "ridgetop to ridgetop" approach, covering the entire valley. "We must honor the covenant. We have a covenant with our Creator: take care of the land and it will take care of you. Everything is connected, and we must work hand-in-hand to focus on not just one part, but the whole ecosystem."

Phyllis Collyer has influenced Bonners Ferry for most community members' lives. She owned a local dry cleaning business for many years, and has worked as a seamstress from her home on the south side of town for decades. "I will be sewing until my fingers don't work anymore," she says.

Phyllis moved to Boundary County from Moscow, Idaho with her family during the Great Depression, when she was only a year old. As a child, she attended Northside Elementary School (currently Northside Bed and Breakfast) and Southside High School. Phyllis has fond memories of her childhood on the Northside. Her family had no car until she went to high school, but thankfully, the grocery store was near her home. She recalls having to cross the old narrow bridge to get to town. It was full of gaps and often surrounded by rushing water. Phyllis' favorite memories of those days in Bonners Ferry include meeting Santa on the sidewalk as a child, seeing the post office being built in the 1930's, and watching the construction of the city's overpass.

One local resident remembers, "When we were children, Phyllis lived in the neighborhood where everything was going on. Everyone knew her. From the time we were little, she was hemming our skirts or pants before school." On the weekends, she was an active member of the Bonners Ferry Boat Club, camping with her family at Smokey Acres.

When asked if she had any concerns for Boundary County, Phyllis said her greatest worries stem from the growth and changes she has seen in recent years, particularly the influence of drugs in the community. She stated, "I hope Bonners Ferry doesn't get too big. I want it to stay Bonners Ferry."

Richard Hollenbeck was born and raised in Bowman, North Dakota, but migrated with his parents and seven siblings to Washington during the Dust Bowl. Richard went on to establish his own family in the Pacific Northwest with his wife, Elsie, and he's now a grandfather and great-grandfather. He still has one sister, but the rest of the North Dakota family has since passed.

From 1958-1960, Richard served in the Army in Fort Lee, Virginia. He attended Eastern Washington University and played football there. He later earned a Master's Degree in General Education at Gonzaga University.

He came to Bonners Ferry in 1960 and taught school for 35 years at both Valley View Elementary and the old high school. Richard coached football for four years, after which, he says, he "fished for ten years" before eventually returning to coaching. In addition to coaching, Richard taught speech and health classes at Bonners Ferry High School for many years.

Richard notes that much has changed in the downtown area during the time he's lived here. The old Safeway building used to be a hay distributor and Akin's Harvest Foods was an International farm dealer. However, he believes in looking forward as well as back and has ideas for future city improvements. One of these is a hope for city planners to attract businesses that offer more jobs.

Richard has been an active member of a number of community organizations, including Shriners, Masons, and Friends of the Restorium. He also contributes time to volunteer work, serving on the City Transportation Committee and the County Waterways Committee. And certainly, anyone who has ever been to the Boundary County Fair has heard Richard's "pickle siren" announcing every pickle sold at his booth.

As if all that wasn't enough, though, Richard remains "Coach" to many and will always be known as the man with the strongest hugs in the county.

꙳꙳꙳

Elsie Hollenbeck has contributed to Boundary County for most of her life. She grew up in Spokane County, where her family owned a dairy farm. After high school, she earned her Bachelor's degree at Eastern Washington University and her Masters in Education at Gonzaga University. In 1960, Elsie moved to Bonners Ferry and began a 35-year teaching career. During that time, she taught fifth and sixth grade, middle school language arts, seventh grade girls' physical education, and high school physical education. The multiple generations who passed through her classroom doors all testify to her deep commitment to serving and educating local families.

Elsie remembers the school culture of the 1960's as being much different from today's when she began teaching. In fact, back then, because women were required to wear skirts and dresses, Elsie was not allowed to wear pants to school. She counts her first teaching job as one of her topmost memorable life events, ranking it beside memories of watching her own children grow.

Elsie recalls other changes that Bonners Ferry has undergone since she arrived. She described it as a formerly Democrat-leaning timber and farming town that has transformed to the more conservative town it is today. One of the biggest changes Elsie notes is the transition of the Bonners Ferry community into what she refers to as an "older person community." She expresses a few concerns over the decreasing number of younger families settling in the area. She believes that a progressive culture would support growth and changes that benefit the area as a whole. As our younger citizens leave Bonners Ferry, there are fewer people to support the infrastructure of the town and the schools that help to build it.

Along with stronger community support for current and future schools, Elsie says she would like to see the local community take advantage of the numerous recreational opportunities the beautiful Boundary County provides year-round.

Former mayor Darrell Kerby was born and raised in Bonners Ferry and attended all twelve grades at local schools. During his sophomore year he fell in love with Patty, the high school sweetheart who eventually became his wife. He has two adult daughters, Kelly and Dawn, and one grandson, Kerby. Darrell attended University of Idaho to become a teacher and later obtained his M.S. at Gonzaga University. As a young man, he took over his father's half interest in an insurance and real estate company, Pace Kerby Agency, which he still owns and operates.

Darrell feels that the opportunities and experiences made available to him through community involvement have been a privilege. He became a member of Bonners Ferry City Council at the age of 24, and has been serving the area ever since. As mayor, the revitalization of downtown Bonners Ferry, along with the infrastructure necessary to support it, marked what he believes to be one of his chief accomplishments. Reaching beyond the local community, Darrell has represented the interests of Idaho as well, serving as a state senator during the 2010 legislative session.

In addition to membership in the Shriners organizations and the local Rotary club, Darrell has served on a number of boards, including Kaniksu Health Services, Boundary Economic Development Council, and Kootenai Valley Resource Initiative. He is currently Chairperson of the Idaho Health and Welfare Board. He has been recognized by local, state, and national agencies for his commitment and excellence.

Darrell values the farming and logging industries, and he cites a number of local farmers, loggers, and industry leaders for their progressive practices and utilization of renewable resources in this community. "When a hometown Bonners Ferry boy gets involved, he has so many more possibilities to be heard and make connections with influential people. I have had these opportunities, as have several others from Bonners Ferry. It helps to make changes."

Sandy Ashworth grew up near Oakland, California, which was a smaller town during her childhood. As Oakland grew and became more urban, Sandy chose to leave her California ranch and move to North Idaho. Sandy recalls, "A very memorable moment for me was coming to Bonners Ferry and seeing how beautiful it was."

Many changes have occurred in the Kootenai Valley since Sandy's arrival all those decades ago. Back then, the number of small businesses in town was large enough that locals could "pretty well get what they needed within a walking distance." Although a stay-at-home mom for years, Sandy and her husband went on to own several small businesses in Bonners Ferry, including a cedar shake mill and a Sears catalog store.

Sandy also remembers a time when a large number of rural residents lived from the resources provided by the land, logging in the winter and farming in the summer. She recalls how that changed, however, when the public acquisition of a large percentage of county land combined with the Endangered Species Act of 1973 to cause some significant restrictions on the local timber and agricultural industries.

Sandy began working at the Boundary County Library in 1985, and has been working there ever since. In 2002, she received the Museum and Library Services National Award, which recognized the Boundary County Library as a leader for its role in the life of our small town. For the past few years, Sandy has partnered with a number of educational institutions and services, working on a project to expand the library and encourage innovation in Boundary County. Although the levy for the expansion of the library did not pass in recent elections, she has made significant progress on a project called the Fab Lab, in partnership with the Massachusetts Institute of Technology. A Fab Lab expands learning with new equipment like 3D printers, metal lathes, and oscilloscopes for new business starters and inventors. It will offer Bonners Ferry the opportunity to apply data to innovate, integrating the latest technology for practical application.

Sandy envisions a bright tomorrow for Bonners Ferry, which is why she is investing so much in it now.

Ron Smith has been an influential member of the Boundary County community for over 30 years. He was born in Kentucky and raised in New Jersey until the age of twelve, then moved back to Kentucky to with his family. After graduating from high school, he joined the Air Force and was stationed in Spokane when he met his wife. They married three months later.

When he left the Air Force, Ron returned to Kentucky, where he first worked at Warren County jail, then later as a police officer. He and his wife moved to Bonners Ferry in 1979 when his father-in-law was struggling with Parkinson's disease.

Upon his return to Bonners Ferry, he found himself working in law enforcement once again, this time with the Boundary County sheriff's department. He regarded his sheriff's position as "connecting with the community while enforcing the law." After six years in that capacity, he changed careers to work at Rocky Mountain Academy. While there, he was elected to a county commissioner position and later left RMA to devote himself fully to public office. He served as County Commissioner for 16 years. During those years Ron also began his involvement in Bonners Ferry High School as an active Badger Booster, contributing financially and also volunteering during local high school sporting events.

Ron supports the local school programs because he loves to have a hand in helping young people achieve their goals. He hopes that all youth and interested residents take advantage of higher education and the county's scholarship program. Ron cites his family as his greatest accomplishment and prides himself in the success of his own children.

It seems natural, then, for Ron to state that his favorite thing about Bonners Ferry is its great number of kind and friendly people. Among his wishes for Boundary County, Ron would like to see a revival of the timber industry. He has shown concern for building and sustaining local jobs, and he knows that those serving the county have the best interests of the community in mind. Ron appreciates the opportunities he's had to serve, saying, "I have enjoyed every minute."

Although Carolyn Testa grew up in New York, she has invested in this community since she fell in love with North Idaho on a camping trip in 1998. Carolyn left her real estate career in Atlanta to move to Bonners Ferry in 2006. From that time she has spearheaded community events, restoration projects, and business ventures that have brought renewed energy and life to the town.

One of Carolyn's first renovation projects, The Groove Studio, fills a niche beyond local arts and crafts co-ops. As an artist, Carolyn recognized a need for a local art gallery and dreamed of a space with slat walls for hanging and showcasing a variety of art media. Following the Downtown Renovation Project, she purchased the former bank building on the corner of Kootenai and Main Streets and invested in creating a gallery that houses local art for the community to experience. Initially, Carolyn did not display her own art; encouraged by friends, she now exhibits her own work, offering her unique style, talent, and imagination.

Several years after opening The Groove Studio, Carolyn envisioned another dynamic project. She renovated an old church and introduced The Pearl Theater, Bonners Ferry's first community theater for the performing arts. Established in 2012, The Pearl offers opportunities for people interested in performing arts of all kinds to share and experience local, national, and international performers. The non-profit's mission is "to foster the performing arts throughout Boundary County for the education, entertainment, and inspiration of the community."

In addition to projects for the arts, Carolyn enjoys community building events, including the Turkey Trot fun run, First Fridays, Summertime Sundays, and Chili Cook-Off, to name just a few. Without seeking personal recognition, she has given of herself wholeheartedly to the Boundary County community, invigorating the town's business cooperation, artistic spirit, and community pride.

☙ ☙ ☙

Tim Wilson, born and raised in Boundary County, is a third generation attorney, carrying on his family's traditions in the military and law. His grandfather first came to practice law in North Idaho after graduating from Colorado Law School. Tim's parents grew up here and, after serving in World War II, his father returned to work as a lawyer. Tim attended Bonners Ferry High School, where he wrestled and played football. He attended Boise State University in 1974, when it was a brand new institution, and he joined the Marines after finishing college.

As a Marine Corps fighter pilot, Tim flew side-by-side with the first female fighter pilots. He was selected to fly an F4, escorting bombers through Japan. He later flew in the first mission of Desert Storm, where he "learned a whole new definition of fear." He went on to fly 40 combat missions and became an air officer in Somalia after Desert Storm. He also flew fifteen combat missions in Iraq. Tim logged 368 carrier landings and take-offs, with 100 of them on the U.S.S. Roosevelt, making him a Carrier Centurion. At the end of his military career, he became a trial lawyer.

Tim loves Bonners Ferry for its privacy and varied environment, calling it "the essence of freedom." He owns an organic ranch with his wife and believes that Bonners Ferry has made significant improvements in the transportation and logging industries. He also notes improved relations with the Kootenai Tribe. He appreciates the diversity of local businesses now compared to earlier days when, "Bonners used to be all bars and grocery stores." He also remembers a time when locals had to worry about floods every year—something the construction of the Libby Dam greatly minimized in the 1970's.

Although Tim sees a need for more local industries to promote growth, he also sees much progress in Boundary County's future. Tim encourages the people of Boundary County to be willing to embrace new ideas, and to "get out now and see the world because it might not be as easy to do in 20 years."

Local midwife Barb Rawlings moved to the area in 1978 in a back-to-the-land movement. She was born in Kansas City and lived there until she married. She recalls the time when, while looking for the perfect place to raise a family, she drove into Bonners Ferry, saw its stunning beauty, peace, and quiet and immediately realized she was home.

Barb began working at Rocky Mountain Academy in 1986, and she and her husband Paul worked as two of the first staff members to start Boulder Creek Academy in the 1990's. She also took on duties at Northwest Academy, continuing her line of work at those schools for a total of 28 years. She taught CPR and First Aid classes for much of that time, bringing her practical experiences from the field into her faculty and staff training sessions.

Barb became a midwife 40 years ago, after birthing two of her children in a hospital and concluding that families should be given the option to birth at home. She entered the field of midwifery tentatively at first, but when she realized she was naturally gifted to work with delivering mothers, she stepped into her practice with confidence. She trained through apprenticeship, formal and informal study, and became the first Licensed Midwife (LM) in Idaho in 2010.

As a midwife, Barb attends to a woman during pregnancy, childbirth, and up to six weeks afterward. She also collaborates with local physicians to provide the best possible care for her patients. Barb's skill and success over the years have resulted in a raised awareness of midwifery in this area. Recently, the mayor of Bonners Ferry issued a proclamation to celebrate Midwives' Day for Boundary County.

She reflects on the many changes Bonners Ferry has undergone through the years—more traffic and trains, more faces she doesn't recognize, new businesses and more recreational opportunities. Noting that the economy has always had its ups and downs, she states, "It has never been great and probably never will be."

Additionally, Barb says she has a wish for the community to someday become more liberal. Her other hopes include more medical access, as well as a sounder economy and more opportunities for young people. Barb is just as liberal with her giving heart as she is with her politics. She sees herself as a "lifeguard for life—not teaching people how to swim, but making sure they're safe."

Tim Dillin's family has been farming in Boundary County since 1924. Born and raised in Bonners Ferry, Tim graduated in 1977 and served in the Air Force and Army National Guard for a total of 22 years. Tim likes the lifestyle and people of the local area, saying, "It's just a good place to raise a family." He enjoys mountain activities such as hunting, fishing, and snowmobiling. He was also an active member of 4-H as a kid, raising pigs and beef to earn money. He encouraged his own children to move away for a time, so that they could return to appreciate the aspects of small-town life that they may have taken for granted.

As a fourth-generation farmer, Tim is well-known for his innovative farming techniques, buying one of the first minimum-till auto tractors, including GPS guidance, and using new communications systems to stay up-to-date with the markets that impact his business. He's been the president of the Boundary County Grain Growers, an Idaho grain production association with both political and economic ties. The Governor nominated Tim as Idaho Barley Commission President for six years, a group that promotes grower education and research. He also served on the Boundary County Republican Committee, as well as serving on the U.S. Grain Council, where he traveled to Japan, South America, Taiwan and South Korea.

In spite of the timber industry decline, Tim states that farming has remained a constant in Boundary County. He would like to see some population and small business growth, but he also hopes Bonners will retain its small-town feel. Like many others who grew up in the area, Tim says he recognized practically everyone when he was little, but now he sees many strangers. Tim also sees the need for education to improve: "We need to keep kids in school longer. Without a good education system, you can't attract business."

Alva Baker has contributed to Boundary County for most of his life. Born and raised in Bonners Ferry, he graduated from B.F.H.S. in 1951. He was actively involved in Boy Scouts of America for ten years before being drafted in the army and sent to Germany. Upon his return to the States, Alva returned to scouting. He spent 40 years as a Scout Master, during which time he trained 54 Eagle Scouts and mentored hundreds of troops. He taught them hiking, fishing, and outdoor skills, and guided them as they earned merit badges. A majority of the Eagle Scouts he trained have found success, including his two sons and one grandson, who have all carried on the family tradition by earning that prestigious rank. His wife, Peach, says of Alva, "He loves scouting, he lives scouting, he is scouting."

Alva has seen tremendous change in Bonners Ferry. He appreciates the Bonners Ferry of the past, and he mentioned missing his favorite hardware store. He disagrees with the "progress" that has been made and says that if he could have his wish, "politicians would stop being politicians." At the same time, he observes the Bonners Ferry youth leaving the area at increasing rates and attributes this to a lack of job opportunities.

Alva has committed himself to bettering the lives of the younger generations in Bonners Ferry. His graduating class of '51 continues to raise money for a scholarship fund, earning no less than $750 a year for four high school seniors seeking higher education. He enjoys working with the local youth, saying, "It keeps us young." He proves this by still going on camping trips, one in which he takes a group of boys ages 11-18 to Camp Easton for an entire week. Even though he retired from being a Scout Master, he remains involved as Unit Commissioner, though he much prefers the time he spends with the boys at camp.

He maintains that scouting should be about improving lives, not changing people.

Sue Wilson has spent much of her life educating and protecting the people in Boundary County. Her roles as former teacher and retired U.S. Customs and Border Protection officer offered her the perfect platforms from which to serve the people who live here. Recalling memories of her childhood, Sue reflects on the freedom she felt living in a small town. She says that in some ways, little has changed in Bonners Ferry. It's a safe place to live, and while she wants businesses to grow, she hopes it will always retain its small-town feel.

Sue graduated from Bonners Ferry High School and attended the University of Idaho, majoring in Physical Education with a minor in Health. She spent four years teaching fourth to twelfth grade Physical Education in Wyoming, then returned to Bonners Ferry to be closer to her family. In 1984, Sue was hired for a seasonal position with U.S. Customs to handle the increasing visitors for the Los Angeles Olympics.

After 30 years in Customs, Sue retired and began to focus on her passions—photography and the arts. As the president of the Pearl Theatre, she stays involved with a number of community volunteers and entertainment groups. The Pearl has a variety of artistic performances, including children's choir, various theater productions, open-mic nights and dance recitals. Sue is also a semi-professional photographer who enjoys sharing the natural beauty of the area with her friends and neighbors. She hopes to display more of her art and eventually include it in The Groove Studio. Her closeup photographs of wild and dangerous animals showcase her adventurous personality. In addition to hiking and photography, Sue also finds delight in taking hot air balloon rides, describing the experience as "feeling like standing still, as if I'm not even in the air."

Sue reports with a smile, "I don't regret any decisions I've made in my life." It's easy to see why.

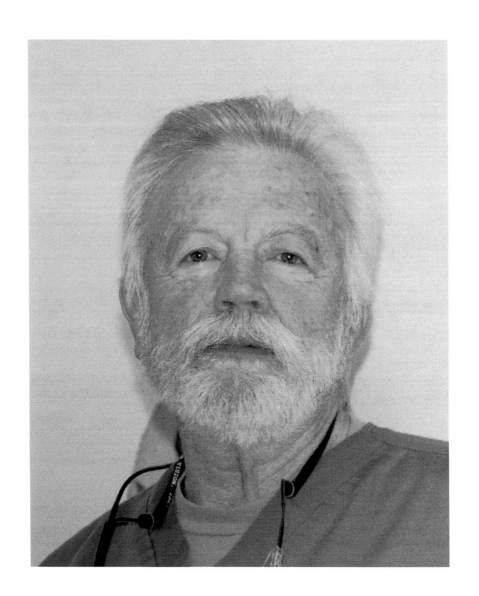

Dr. David McIntosh, D.D.S. grew up in Lincoln, Nebraska, but has lived in a variety of places—from Missouri, to Texas, to Oklahoma and California—before settling in Bonners Ferry in 1978. Seizing the opportunity to travel to the West at various times throughout his youth, he eventually settled in California to practice dentistry. But when the growth rate there shot up quickly, he came to a point where he says "he barely recognized the place," and decided to settle in a town with a slower growth rate.

Dr. McIntosh chose to work in a health related field as a matter of course. He attributes his health-conscious lifestyle to the influence of his family's adherence to Seventh Day Adventist lifestyle practices. As a young man, he considered studying medicine until an influential teacher inspired him to pursue a career in education. That pursuit changed, however, when he became frustrated with trying to transmit his passion for science to students who seemed completely disinterested. Returning to medicine, he then entered the field of dentistry after seeing how its consistent working schedule allowed for more free time to explore the outdoors.

Dr. McIntosh enjoys serving the community. He spent a few years actively involved in the Chamber of Commerce and a number of years as a member of Boundary County Concerned Citizens environmental group. He is presently a member of the Rotary Club. It's hard to believe him when he says he was once a shy person who was afraid to speak up in groups. Now he seems the life of the party, talking and joking freely. Dr. McIntosh says that the confidence he gained from years of having no choice but to talk to others has freed him from worrying over who might be listening.

His advice? Get involved in the community, take the time to sit down and decide if you are truly happy, and always do good for others.

ख ख ख

Judy Dirks was born in Topeka, Kansas and moved with her husband, Larry, to Bonners Ferry in 1961. She met Larry at Kansas City Medical Center where she worked full-time as a registered nurse. Her interest in the health care profession remains to this day as she shares her excitement over the promising work taking place in the medical field, in particular, stem cell research.

For years, Judy has been involved in local volunteer activities and organizations. She's an active member of the Community Coalition for Families and also of the United Methodist Church. Not only does Judy voice her concern for the struggling people of Boundary County, she demonstrates it through her actions. A few ways that she "walks the walk" includes organizing the annual Crop Walk for hunger, as well as advocating for seniors and less fortunate people through her work with the community kitchen. Judy has a knack for inspiring others to give of themselves with volunteer activities, too. She shares a particular interest in racial justice. Upon coming here, she felt surprised to find the lack of racial diversity and acceptance. In this regard, Judy says that Bonners Ferry has changed greatly over the years.

If Judy could change one aspect of Boundary County, she says she would want to see more people exercising their freedom to vote. Having witnessed low voter turnout during the many years she has worked at local elections (with only thirty percent of the population voting much of the time), Judy worries that election results sometimes falsely represent the interests of the community.

However, she does see promise in the areas of economic and educational advancement for the Bonners Ferry area through the development of the Fab Lab. She especially hopes that local citizens will begin to grasp just how much benefit the whole community derives from the investment of money into our local schools and education projects.

For the past 14 years, Dan Dinning has been a Boundary County commissioner who isn't afraid of controversy. He says, "I became a County Commissioner to help the community maintain and grow the natural resource jobs that the lands provide, while seeking to restore health of the landscape....It is my hope that my children, and many future generations will reap the benefit of what we are doing today, that they may share this place with their own families just as I have been able to do."

Dan was born and raised in Boundary County. His family settled in North Idaho in the 1930's, but his wife, Mary, traces her Boundary County roots back even further. Her relatives first arrived in the late 1800's and settled in the Porthill area. Dan and Mary both graduated from Bonners Ferry High School, as did all three of their children. Dan says that he's related in one way or another to "practically everyone here."

Dan first came to light as a local politician when he turned his attention to public lands issues, at times risking his popularity for his beliefs. As an active member of the Kootenai Valley Resource Initiative, he works with the Kootenai Tribe and a number of private and public entities to restore and maintain social, cultural, economic, and natural resources. He is also the Chair of Idaho Association Counties Natural Resource Litigation fund, and has been working with other counties and with the state government to maintain sustainable forestry practices in Idaho.

He believes that differing opinions on issues don't need to stifle the decision-making process. "We can all learn from each other, even those we disagree with. The KVRI is made up of people who uphold sometimes opposite viewpoints, but we've learned how to work through those differences and produce sensible, workable solutions that none of us could have come up with as individuals."

Dan advises people in the community with these words: "Life has many doors; don't be afraid to knock. If a door doesn't answer, knock again." He especially encourages the younger generation to never give up. He certainly didn't.

ACKNOWLEDGMENT:

We wish to express our heartfelt thanks to the people we interviewed for this book and to all those who assisted us in our marketing and distribution efforts. We are moved by the openness and generosity we encountered at every turn in Bonners Ferry. This little town will always occupy a special place in our hearts.

–Boulder Creek Academy Service Learning Students, 2015

Made in United States
Troutdale, OR
11/24/2024